DOG INSPIRED LESSONS

Heart-warming insights on forgiveness, letting go, and loving unconditionally.

This is Cooper's second starring role. He is the inspiration for a fictional dog, aptly named Cooper, in *Walk-In Investigations: Streaming Sarah, A Paranormal Detective Mystery*. Cooper is the trusty sidekick of Detective Katie Hanson, a psychic detective.

Copyright 2017 Interacting Worlds Press
Cover revised July 2017.
No change to the interior
Cover Design: SelfPubBookCovers.com/ LadyLight
ISBN: 978-0-692-84732-9 (paperback)
Library of Congress Control Number: 2017902507
Joyce Kostakis, Clackamas, OR

DEDICATION

To Cooper and Max, thank you for sharing your joy and inspiring me to be a better person.

Thank you Dyan Bourne for providing the Belget puppy photo.

Special thanks to Robin Peralta, Laura Hunter, Nancy Naizer, Evelyn Holland, and Darla Carpenter for taking time out of their busy schedules to give me their valuable feedback and insights I couldn't have done it without you.

CHAPTER ONE: Attention

I have shared my life with numerous pets over the years and learned valuable lessons from every one of them. My heart is bursting with the unconditional love that animals have somehow mastered despite past abandonment, trauma, and horrific abuse.

I was blessed to have cats, dogs, hamsters, rabbits, and even a few horny toads growing up. Growing up having my sweet Lab to turn to when I needed to share my deepest thoughts, fears, and embarrassing moments was cathartic. I was loved unconditionally, no matter what I shared. There was no judgment; no chance that he would use it against me later during a heated argument.

My secrets were as safe as if they were locked in a vault at Ft. Knox. His warm, comforting gaze told me everything was going to be okay; his wag said it wasn't as bad as all that, and his head resting gently on my lap meant he felt my pain and was there for me.

As an adult, I settled on having both cats and dogs at the same time. Watching them coexist is always a reminder that we can all get along, no matter what our differences, no matter what baggage full of past hurts we have dragged into the relationship.

I have no doubt that each pet who shared their lives with me was God-guided into my life. It is perfect that dog is God spelled backward; it gives a dual meaning when I share the dog-guided inspirational stories that taught me profound lessons in love, living in the moment, gratitude, and the power of forgiving and letting go. If you ask me, these God-guided pups are angels on this earth, watching over us, keeping us safe, and, if we watch closely, they are invaluable teachers. This book is dedicated to each one with love and gratitude for the many lessons, and I give them special thanks for graciously and patiently accepting me as their fur mom.

I will admit that I learned lessons from all of my pets. So why are Max & Cooper the stars of this book? Why are their experiences noteworthy? I'm not sure if it is because they are the ones currently in my life or that their characters so closely resemble my husband's and my personality, which I didn't connect until I saw a comment on a photo I posted on Facebook.

"I see who takes after who."

That comment stayed with me and I started to notice how our personalities were similar to Cooper's and Max's characters. My friend nailed it. Max, the small brown one, had my personality, and Cooper had my husband's more laid-back and calm personality.

One day, I couldn't believe how gentle Cooper was with Max. Max was acting like a real toot, trying to push Cooper's buttons to get him to play. Cooper didn't want to play but, instead of snapping at Max about how busy he was and didn't have time to play, he pretended that Max overpowered him and he laid down while Max assumed the winner's pose. Having won, Max trotted off to look out the window and Cooper had his downtime.

I realized how much I could learn from Cooper and Max and how we could all take a page from their book. Now I think of Cooper and Max as not only extended members of the family, but they are my God-guided dogs … ever ready to present daily reminders of forgiveness, the power of letting go, and the beauty of living life in the moment.

I had more than my share of moments when I shut someone down with a not-now-I'm-busy glare or comment. I decided to apply what I learned while watching Cooper and Max interact on a day-to-day basis.

I put my plan into action. I was going to give my full attention if someone needed it, even if it was for only a few moments. My goal was not to push them away, and not to feel frustrated or pulled on by the request.

I work from home and when I've been staring at the computer for a few hours not even blinking, Max will make his way to my desk and then pop his head up from under the desk and climb on my chair. In the past, I would push him back down with a firm "not now I'm busy." Following Cooper's example of not pushing Max away when he needs a little play, I decided these were opportunities to take a stretch break and to get a glass of water. Now, I grab my water, give Max a scratch, open the back door so he can do a quick run in the yard. I enjoy the view for a few minutes and head back to my desk. It's done wonders for helping me keep my water goal each day, and a quick stretch break helps me take a deep breath and has a calming effect when I get back at it. And Max either entertains himself with a toy he found in the yard or gets fascinated by a squirrel and is happy and content. He didn't need hours of my time, just a moment or two to feel like he mattered and to know that I remembered he was an important part of my life. Isn't that worth a few moments?

  I tried as best I could to mirror their behavior. The result was positive. I feel emulating the pups has taught me how to be a better person. It has taught me to be a better friend, coworker, sister, wife, and pet owner. I'm not going to lie; I still have the occasional taste of green-pea soup rising to the surface. There are days I'm in the running for the Exorcist award as my head spins and I snap at a loved one, but I'd like to think I'm much lower on the list of honorable mentions.

  I decided to write this book to share my insights as well as provide a few photos to give you a smile in the process. The chapters that follow are either an insight that I received by watching Cooper and Max or gentle reminders to put something I already knew back into practice.

CHAPTER TWO: Leap of Faith

My dog Monty passed unexpectedly. He was such a special dog. I knew I belonged to him the moment I saw him playing with his litter-mates at Hearts & Paws Doggie Daycare. I picked him up, and he took a big sigh and relaxed into my neck. He did that every time I picked him up over the next six weeks until he was old enough to adopt. He and my Lab Summer were inseparable for the next ten years. We were shaken to the core when he died. Summer was hit especially hard. We decided to adopt another pup to help her through her grief.

The search for Summer's new brother was an easy one. Unfortunately, there are no shortages of abandoned animals. We had several local shelters, and they were all online. I went through each of the photos and, when I saw Cooper's smile, it caught my breath and my heart skipped a beat. That is his adoption photo above. Isn't that the sweetest smile? I knew he was the perfect one for our family just as sure as I knew I belonged to Monty the day I picked him up and he collapsed into my neck. My husband and I went to a few shelters to see a handful of pups we both liked from the virtual shelter photos. I saved Cooper for last because I knew he was coming home with us.

His name at the shelter was L.C., a name picked by one of the staff members. I didn't want him associating his name with the shelter so I called him Cooper. Not sure why … it just seemed to fit. It was close to closing time when we arrived at the shelter. They brought him out to a fenced-in meet-and-greet area and I fell in love. He was such a gentle soul. My husband raced home to get Summer so the two could meet on neutral ground. They ran around the yard together with no issues. Summer had a new brother!

We took Cooper home and that is when the lesson on forgiveness, letting go, and living in the moment started. Unlike a dating site where you can take the time to get to know a person before you start a relationship, pet adoption is quite the opposite. It is a leap of faith; a dive right in and a hope that the water doesn't give you a heart attack. Sure there was the 30-minute meet-and-greet, but nothing akin to months of instant messaging, meeting for lunch and dinner, and then eventually settling into a cozy relationship or running for the hills.

We discovered Cooper had some emotional baggage, as we all do, and he dragged it into our relationship, as most of us do. He was no different than a person holding on to past hurts and fears as he dipped his toe into the new relationship waters. We will never know his history or his trauma. Our role was to help him through it, to have patience, and show him that a life of love and trust is possible.

So what happened to the lovable pup we met at the shelter? Was he bipolar? Did he have a split personality? The Cooper we met in the meet-and-greet yard was not the Cooper that walked into the house with us. Correction: he was the same Cooper that walked into the house, just not the same when he walked out of the house. Our lovable Cooper had leash aggression, and he had it badly. The day he met Summer, they were both off-leash in a fenced-in area; hence, the sweet Cooper. During our first walk together, we got to meet the Tasmanian-devil Cooper.

If Cooper saw another dog within 25 feet, he would spin in circles, jaw flapping, teeth snapping, and then he would lunge for the other dog. If your knee was anywhere near his snapping jaws, you were hit. He didn't mean to bite; he was coming from a place of deep fear. It took one year of love and patience and five different trainers before we were able to reach him.

That is sweet Cooper below (on a leash) sitting next to strangers, relaxed and happy as can be.

If there were one behavior I had to pick to emulate from Cooper, it would be forgiving and letting go. He was able to put his past behind him, let go of his fears, live in the moment, and make new friends in the process.

CHAPTER THREE: Listen When God Comes Calling

In 2014, Summer passed away and my heart was broken, as was Cooper's. I wasn't ready to adopt another pup. We were planning a move to Oregon in a few months and the thought of two dogs and three cats in the car for three days made me shudder.

I tried to hold fast. Cooper repeatedly gave me his I'm-lonely-and-need-a-friend eyes. Anyone with a beloved pet knows those eyes... the ones that constantly say, "I just need someone to play with me!" I asked him to be patient and promised him I would adopt a friend when we got to Oregon. He refused to hear it.

If ever there were a God-guided "tail," Max is it. Apparently, Cooper had turned to God with his request, since his efforts to sway me were falling on deaf ears. What do I mean? A few weeks after the daily stare down, a stray dog (Max) found his way to our front door. I will admit that I added to the prayer as well, so I guess you could say we tag teamed our request. So here is the lowdown on how Max joined the family and how I changed my position about waiting until we moved.

    I guess Cooper asked God to put Max in our path when we were on our walk that day. I added to the request to bring Max into our family as soon as I saw him with my neighbor during our walk. We stopped to talk. I asked her if he was her new pup and she told me he lived in the neighborhood and she was tired of taking him home. My neighbor said that she was going to give the owner a good tongue-lashing and if she saw the pup loose again, she would take him to the pound because she didn't want him to get run over.

    I knew Max was the one for us at that moment. At that time, Cooper was over his leash-aggressive behavior, but he would still get nervous if a strange dog got too close. Cooper didn't react to Max at all. He just sat and watched us while we were all talking. Not even a nervous lip lick. We were leaving for Greece the next day and I wasn't in a position to take Max in. I put a prayer request to God's ear that I would be willing to take Max when I got back. I added that if he was meant to be in our family, when I returned from Greece to put him back in my path and I would take care of the rest. I kid you not, we returned late on a Friday evening and very early Saturday morning I saw something sitting outside my front door. I opened the door and it was a cold, soaking wet Max.

Well, I asked God to put him in my path if it was meant to be; I just didn't think he would ring my doorbell. I called out to my husband to put Cooper on a leash and bring him out front. I told my husband if they got along, we should ask the owners if we could keep him. "Just like that?" my husband asked. When it is meant to be, yes, just like that.

Cooper and Max hit it off immediately. I brought Max in and they took a nap on the couch together. When the rain stopped, I took Max and Cooper on their first walk together to ask the owner if we could keep him. The owner looked relieved and told me the dog was a pain in the #%#$ and, yes, I could keep him.

"Anything I should know?" I asked. "He likes to eat old shoes," was the response. I'm sure you can see the thought bubble pop up over my head. What? Old shoes? My guess was all shoes were fair game, and I loved my shoes. "How does he know the difference between an old shoe and a new one?" I asked, knowing there was no difference to the pup. "All my shoes are old," he replied. "One more thing," I asked. "If Max doesn't get along with my cats, can I bring him back?" "Of course," was the response.

I think we both knew that Max wasn't coming back. It turns out Max thinks he is a cat. As you can see, we had no issues. I'm glad I asked for Max to come into our lives. We are the richer for it.

CHAPTER FOUR: Loving unconditionally

Loving unconditionally isn't an impossible task. In relationships, like our pets, we start off loving unconditionally, and have every intention of loving until "death do us part". In the beginning, it's easy to love everything about your mate, especially when you have love-endorphins coursing through your body. You want to do anything to please each other. But once the love endorphins simmer down, which is usually at the two-year mark and then life happens, you get busy, you get distracted, and distance starts to build. The "until death do us part" starts to feel far off. Love is no longer measured by the number of butterflies in our stomach at the expectation of seeing the other, but instead, it is measured by the number of expectations and demands that are fulfilled. Did they take out the trash as you asked? If the answer is yes, then you feel loved. If it is no, then you might feel that your significant other doesn't care enough to help you out.

Close your eyes and remember how you felt making your significant other delight at a sweet gesture like leaving a note in their briefcase or purse or surprising them with their favorite treat you picked up at the store. You thought of them and took the time to let them know it.

There is no doubt that you still love your mate even when you are frustrated that they leave the counter messy with all of their hair products or the socks never seem to hit the hamper. They know you still love them as well. It just gets harder for them to recognize that love through the glare or frown as you pick up the socks or sweep the items off the counter into an open drawer. It might be oversimplifying, but not having the expectation that your mate has the same pet peeve of a spotless floor or counter as you do reduces the irritation when you see the socks next to the hamper or the pile of hair products on the counter. I read a short story recently where a woman would always nag at her husband for leaving his clothes in a trail on the way to bed. It was a real sore spot with her until he passed and then she missed that trail of clothes. Think about the little things that drive you crazy.

Would you do anything to have those back if your mate was no longer with you?

CHAPTER FIVE: Forgiving & Letting Go

And please don't let mom be mad that I ate her new coloring pencils this morning. Amen.

    I shared the story of Cooper's forgiveness and letting go of his trauma. I'm sure we all agree that he had some deep emotional scarring to overcome.

    What about the not so deep, day-to-day hurts? This is the stuff that is seemingly benign but leaves a small emotional cut, and when these cuts build up, they can leave you in a pool of emotional blood (if you let them.)

    I love to color, and for Christmas, I received a stack of coloring books and color pencils with every color imaginable. Yes, it is my fault for leaving my office open and keeping the coloring books and pencils on my desk within reach of Max. I know better, but I must have been distracted and forgot to lock my office door. I say lock because they are French doors and Max just gives the door a high five, and they pop open.

Anyway, I returned from whatever had distracted me. I walked into my office to find most of my new pencils shredded in a pile, like a pack of beavers had taken up residence in my office.

I had a shared responsibility in this outcome. I could have been mad that the white carpet, now multi-colored, was possibly stained beyond the power of the rug cleaner tucked beneath my kitchen cabinet. I could have been mad that the color pencils were now a fraction of the rainbow I had been gifted with. I could have been, but I wasn't. Maybe I was numb to the constant destruction that is Max; maybe I'm at the age now where I realize there are two sides to every story, two parties to every fight. Perhaps in the scheme of things, it was no big deal. My birthday hadn't changed; I still had my health and the world was still spinning.

Had Max taught me perspective or did he just wear me down? I'd like to think it is the former.

So how do you handle the little hurts? I'm talking about how you recover from a coworker's jabbing dig. Or how you react to your mate snapping at you when you ask a simple question. How do you respond to being cut off in traffic? Do you forgive? Or do you speed up and try to jump in front of the offending person and slam on your brakes? Or do you complain about the jerk for a solid hour when you get to work? Do you let the comment from your coworker fester for days and build responses in your head so the next time it happens, you will be ready with a zinger? Or do you let it go, but follow up with some passive-aggressive way of getting back at them?

What if you just let it go altogether? What if you didn't take it personally and saw it as their stuff? What if you recognized it has nothing to do with you. Maybe they are having a bad day, maybe something in what you said brought up some of their old shit and rather than deal with it, they attacked you or they chose to "chew on your new pencils." What if you both just stopped when the hurt happened and acknowledged how that made you feel? Or you sent them love and a prayer that their day turns around?

Watching Max and Cooper play each day is a reminder that hurts can be forgiven without leaving emotional scars and without taking up residence in your baggage of issues. You can let the hurt go the moment it happens, shake it off, and move on.

With Max and Cooper, forgiveness is instant. If one of them plays too hard and hurts the other, there is a quick warning yelp. The other stops and gives an apologetic kiss and they are right back at it. They have mastered forgiveness and the art of letting go. Max doesn't sulk in the corner and glare, and Cooper doesn't attack Max in reaction to accidentally getting nipped. It's like it never happened and they are back to being besties within a second.

I want to follow their example. When I'm stressed and snap at someone as a reaction, I want to stop, acknowledge it, apologize, and hope that we can move on. Obviously, I want to learn not to snap in the first place. I'm working on it but I'm not there yet. In the meantime, I will keep trying; I will keep apologizing.

It is critical to your health and happiness to forgive. Holding a grudge harms you more than the person that hurt you. If you can let go and forgive, you will live a happier and healthier life.

I had a friend that would constantly get mad at people and cut them out of her life. If you asked her to attend a gathering, she had to know the name of everyone going. If anyone was attending who was on her shit list, she wouldn't attend. There was almost always someone on her shit list. How sad for her that she lost out on so many new experiences because of a grudge. And here is the kicker; when you asked her why she was mad at X, she would say, "I don't remember but she really made me mad." She didn't even remember why she was mad. How crazy is that?

At one time or another, we all have made mistakes, said something we wish we could take back, and behaved in a way that we wished we hadn't. We have hurt someone in some way over the course of our lifetime and, like Max with my pencils, sometimes without even realizing we've caused pain. Sadly, some injuries run deeper than others, but we have all been there. We have felt a blow and have dealt a blow. Try to see the other person's side. Where are they coming from? Is the baggage they carry around greater than yours? Could this be the reason some people react the way they do? Take my grudge-holding friend, for example. What "wounded" her so deeply could be a twisted version of what happened; hence, why she can't remember why she is so angry.

None of us are immune to misunderstandings, misinterpretations or misrepresentations, including me. The example I'm about to give may be a bit woo-woo for some of you, but bear with me. You will see where I am going with it.

I remember while growing up that my mom would joke about not having a name for me when they tried to leave the hospital. The nurse stopped my mom and dad when they tried to leave the hospital with me and refused to let them leave until they put a name on my birth certificate. Mom and Dad flipped through a Bible at the Nurse's station and saw my name on the back of a family tree. On the birth certificate it went. When I heard this story, I thought, nice; this is how much thought they put into my name, which made me wonder if they even wanted me. As time went by, I forgot about this story until one day when I was in an emotional release seminar and they asked us to do an exercise where we had to release a past wrong.

They asked us to think of an event that happened to us that hurt us emotionally and that we had not let go of. After something had come to mind, we were to rewrite the story with an ending of our choosing. The goal was energetically imprinting an outcome that you would have preferred (I told you it was out there).

When a person was on the table telling their "story," a facilitator was at the head of the table guiding the new story. I refer to this as the Dr. Phil approach. You know, "how did that make you feel?" or "how would you like to see the ending happen?" Meanwhile, at the foot of the table, an energy worker was sending energy. The theory behind the drill was that memories are stored in our cells and as the cells die and are replaced with new cells, the revised story will imprint on the new cells. The result would be that the old memory would no longer have power over us.

I froze. Nothing came to mind. I always believed that I wouldn't trade anything that happened to me. All my experiences, good or bad, made me who I was and I liked who I was. Suddenly, there it was: my turn. As I climbed on the table, the facilitator asked me what my story was. I heard it at the same time my mouth said it. It was as if it bypassed my brain, skipped the processing filter, and just popped out. I heard myself say, "my parents didn't have a name for me." What the? Where did that come from? I continued to share my "nameless" story. As my story progressed, I heard myself say, "I know I was premature but only by one month. Surely in eight months, they could have come up with some kind of name. I guess they just got too busy." Once my tale of woe ended, I was asked to revise my ending. "Easy enough," I said. "They are filling out the birth certificate with my name while they are laughing and walking out of the hospital."

Both my parents had passed long before I took this seminar. The night of the workshop, I had a dream. I honestly don't know if it was my mom coming through or a repressed memory, but I dreamed that my mom woke me up and told me that they had always had a name for me but, because they were told I was a boy, the name they had chosen was for a boy. It wasn't that they didn't get around to naming me; it was that they had the wrong name picked out. They never thought to have a backup name because everyone was certain I was a boy. Yes, this was before sonograms. I think back then someone hovered a ring over her stomach or felt how "high-up" the baby was. Anyway, making a very short story longer, I woke and sat straight up. I remembered everything. The story flooded to the surface of my mind. I had a total memory of Mom sharing "my name" story with me including not having a girls name. I had forgotten it and had chosen to hold on to my "version." Stopping to think about it now, how many of our "grudges" are our twisted versions of what actually happened? Could we be holding on to something we misinterpreted or twisted based on our misconstrued memories? Is that possible? For certain, having empathy or recognizing that experiences may not have unfolded in the way one remembers doesn't mean you accept the behavior; it just may help to let things go. Learning to let go may help to lead a fuller, happier, and healthier life. After all, isn't that what we all want?

CHAPTER SIX: Having Each Other's Back

When we go for walks or hang out in the yard, I can see Max and Cooper scanning the horizon, looking back at each other, then me, to make sure we are still doing okay. There is always a check-in every few minutes, even if they are deeply focused on some new find. They always watch out for each other.

Ever wonder why your dog wants to hang out with you in the bathroom? It is a thank-you for protecting him on his walk. He knows he can safely stop and "do his business" because he is watching your face for signs of approaching danger. Your pup knows you have his back and he wants to return the favor. And you thought it was just the lovely smell.

My sister and I are besties now, but growing up we used to have intense screaming matches at each other. Mom always made my sister take me with her. Dragging your kid sister around is a pain and tensions ran high. However, no matter how much we yelled at each other, if someone said anything about one of us, the other would come out fighting mad in full defense.

I've been blessed to have loving in-laws and my family adores my husband. I've seen couples get in the biggest fights because they didn't feel supported when they felt attacked or put down by a family member. I think it is important to stand up for each other, especially when it comes to family. I think wedding vows should be love, honor, respect, and support. It's a tough world out there and even tougher when you feel like you are going at it alone. Just knowing you have someone in your life that has your back makes the journey so much smoother.

I see a large number of younger employees frozen to inaction and in need of every decision to be made for them because they are afraid to decide. This is not because they are concerned that the decision is wrong. Everything is recoverable and can be corrected. Sure, sometimes there is a financial cost to the correction, but there is also a lesson in it and an opportunity for growth.

The fear is that their manager won't back them. They are made to feel as if they are empowered to make decisions, but when something goes amuck and leadership screams, you know what rolls downhill. Managers should make it a practice to have their employee's back. It will make for a more cohesive team; it will build trust and provide better customer service.

Then there is the sisterhood. Women are powerful and are a force to be reckoned with, particularly when in a group. If we were more supportive of each other, the world would be a better place. Sometimes we are our own worst enemies and sabotage each other instead of helping each other and building each other up. That doesn't apply to all, but a great many can be catty. I work with a manager that calls it out when it happens and it cracks me up. When she sees women not supporting each other or attacking each other in meetings, she holds up her hand like a claw and says "Meow, kitty likes to scratch." It generates laughter and lightens the tension. We need to embrace the power of the sisterhood and work together. We can do it!

CHAPTER SEVEN: Communication

It is important to keep the lines of communication open. I love watching Max and Cooper communicate. If Max wants to play, he assumes the play-bow position. If Cooper doesn't, he jumps on the couch with me, sending the message that he is not interested, thanks for asking.

Have you noticed there are times when you have such a heavy workload and tight deadlines that you feel charged by it? You hear people say things such as "I work better under pressure." Then there are times with the same workload and deadlines that you feel you are going to snap if one more thing is added to your plate. Why the difference? Is it the feeling of being valued or not valued? We have an innate need to feel appreciated and to know that our contributions matter.

We will dive in and give a task everything we have if we believe we are making a difference. If we feel we are part of a team. Looking outside of ourselves for that validation can leave us feeling slighted if we don't speak up and let our needs be known. If you are feeling frustrated at work, be honest about it but show up with solutions when you do broach the subject. If your relationship needs are not met, spell out what you need. People communicate differently. You may think your message or signals couldn't be any clearer but, more often than not, when you learn to speak in a way that is more explicit to the recipient, you will be surprised to find they are completely shocked to realize you feel a certain way. When you say the same message in their language, it's as if it is the first time they have heard it, even though you feel as if you have been shouting it from the rooftop for years. It's not just a man versus woman style; it is a communication style. *The 5 Love Languages*, by Gary Chapman, is an excellent book for learning how to communicate your needs in a language that can be understood by the recipient.

Cooper and Max not only communicate with each other, they also watch our bodies for indications of our mood. Are they about to get a treat? Are they about to go for a walk? They scan our faces for frowns to measure how our day went. I used to think it was a sign of guilt when Max went into a corner when I walked into a room and found my _____ torn apart and all over the room (I used a blank space because I had so many items to choose from, I couldn't decide).

He didn't feel guilty; he was watching my body language, my leaning in, my frown. He listened to the deep "are you kidding me!" when my eyes first caught a glimpse of the destruction. Don't just listen to your friend, partner, coworker … look at their body language. Are they saying it is okay with their words, but their body looks like you told them they have three weeks to live? Did they hear your message or are they staring at you with a blank expression as if you just said "I decided to take a shuttle to Mars for the weekend and hook up with an alien." Get some feedback if you are not confident you were heard, or if your message didn't come across as you intended. It doesn't have to be an exam or a "tell me what I just said." That would make any brain freeze. Ask what they think about what you said or how they would put it into practice. You can tell from the answer if your message was clear or if there is going to be a rumor at the water cooler on Monday that you are dating an alien from Mars.

CHAPTER EIGHT: Be A Good Listener

It is not enough to keep the lines of communication open. You have to be a good listener. Max and Cooper are always listening. I swear I can be downstairs with the kitchen door closed and they can be upstairs, and they can hear me open the refrigerator or crack open a chip bag. I knew dogs have an excellent sense of smell and hearing, but I didn't think it was on the level of the Six Million Dollar Man or the Bionic Woman.

Unlike Max and Cooper, I don't have the greatest hearing and more times than not, I find myself asking someone to repeat themselves. Hearing is my problem child. I have always known that there is more to hearing than taking in the sounds that pass through your ears. The second prong is being a good listener. Over the years I've heard people say things such as "lean in" so they know you are interested, "nod" so they know you are on the same page with them, or they ask you to make eye contact. There seemed to be a lot of facets to listening. I put most of those nuggets into practice, and I thought I was a good listener.

  I swallowed hard one day when I heard someone make a comment that people listen with the intent of replying and not learning. If ever I was guilty of something, it was listening with the intent of answering. It wasn't that I felt my response would be earth shattering or enlightening; it was more that I wanted to mentally prepare my position on what was said so I wouldn't look like a deer in the headlights if asked. I had an added habit of interrupting because I was afraid of losing my thought if we got too far into the conversation.

  Would losing my view be so bad? Just like when I meditate, thoughts fly through at an alarming rate; does that mean I need to grab them and share them the second they happen? Did I need to share them at all? I ignore them when I meditate so why do I feel the need to make my thoughts known during a conversation? Isn't it better to let it go and stay focused on what is being said? If it comes back, it was meant to be; if it doesn't, c'est la vie.

CHAPTER NINE: No Backseat Driving

Max and Cooper take turns being Alpha. Sometimes Max calls the shots and sometimes it is Cooper. When it switches, they seem to accept the new role with grace. So how does that translate as a lesson? Delegate and let it go! AKA, don't be a backseat driver.

It is a beautiful thing to watch as Cooper and Max work out their roles on a day-to-day or, sometimes, a minute-to-minute basis. If Cooper feels like letting Max take his toy, he allows Max to snatch it from him without so much as a glance. Giving Max the alpha position on occasion builds Max's confidence. Then there are the days when Max is being an overpowering, obnoxious brat and needs a lesson in manners. If he goes to snatch a toy, Cooper covers it and gives a soft growl. Max stops in his tracks. If he tries to wrestle Cooper and Cooper is not in the mood, he sits on Max and game over ... much like you see an older brother sitting on the younger one.

So how do I put this lesson in practice? Sometimes I am the doer, and sometimes I delegate. We can't do it all, even if we hate to admit it. I remember being at a meeting once at a new company. The president asked one of the managers if she could take on an assignment. With a smile and no apology, she told him her plate was full and, if she took that on, she would not be able to give it her full attention and do a quality job. She also pointed out that if she accepted the assignment, several previously assigned deadlines would be missed. He nodded and turned to another employee who took the assignment.

I must have turned white or had a cartoon look on my face (you know the one - eyes bugged out of the head, tongue on the floor, and an "arruuugaaa" horn going off in the background) because after the meeting he approached me and said, "you know you are allowed to say 'no' to a request." Uh, say "no"? In all my years, I was not aware that this was ever a possibility. When did this little gem get added to the rule book? I was in my 40s at the time. I sure could have used this bit of 411 when I stepped into the working world a few decades back. It would have eliminated many nights of working into the early hours trying to meet a deadline. Just say no, huh. That is the easiest step to crossing items off your to-do list. Just say no and don't add them, who knew. The worst that could happen is the request is denied and your "no" response becomes "when do you want that?" Doesn't hurt to try.

So the "no" didn't work this time and a task has been added to your already impossible to accomplish list of things to do. Be open to examining your tasks and organizing them by priority. Decide what has to be done and is immediate, what has to be done but can wait, and what is a nice to have, but the world wouldn't stop spinning if you cross it off your list. This is a critical step in gaining control over the many spinning plates that you can't seem to bring down, tie a bow on, and put away as done. Notice how I said done, not perfect. The key word is "done." Waiting for something to be perfect just leaves it in the air longer than necessary. Nothing is ever perfect. Do your best, fill the requirements of the task, and close it out. Upload it, email it, publish it; whatever the "it" is, just do it and walk away. If something comes up in the future that you missed, give it a tweak and close 'er down again.

There are many ways to get control of your to-do list. Just walk into any bookstore and throw a dart at a book or do a Google search and pick what resonates with you. Delegating was the hardest for me but I'm so thankful I learned it. In fact, one of my direct reports said to me, "man, have you mastered the art of delegating." I know she was sharing that she was being weighed down but, it was a proud moment for me (I hadn't learned the "no" lesson yet or I would have shared it with her).

There is a significant step in delegating that I think most people miss. This applies especially to the perfectionist. When you delegate, it should be the same as bringing it down, tying a pretty bow on it, and crossing it off the list. Give it away 100%. When I first started delegating, I would keep ownership of it. I was a hovercraft. I watched over the person I gave it to, making sure they did it just right (also known as making sure it was done my way, which was, of course, the perfect way, or so I thought).

When the task was done, I would take it back, examine it for perfection, make tweaks, or end up redoing it because the result wasn't what I had in mind. Dear God, delegating was killing me. It added steps and time to getting 'er done. Whose brilliant idea was it to delegate?

I was missing a crucial component. Delegate and release. Trust the person you gave it to and don't be a backseat driver. There are plenty of things on your list that have you at the wheel. Everyone grows and learns when they are empowered to own a task from start to finish. Let it go, shake off the need to have something perfect, and trust that it is getting done. In the beginning, it will be hard and you may want to redo the dishes after your teenager washes them, but will you die of dysentery if the dishes can't be used as surgical instruments?

CHAPTER TEN: Take Time To Play

Photo by Jim Antich

Taking time to play is so important to your health and happiness. I am happy to share that I learned this lesson years ago, but Max and Cooper are daily reminders. I can't stress enough how important this is to every aspect of your life. It affects your health, your relationships, and how you look back on life during your moments of reflection. Do you have fond memories of time spent with friends and family or are you at a point in your life where you thought you had time to play, only to find your health is too poor to enjoy anything?

Which memories do you want to float to the surface? The memories of the amazing experiences you had and the joy you felt when you shared them with loved ones or the memories of late nights with paperwork and deadlines?

I decided I wanted memories of playing and enjoying life. I was surprised that the decision to play turned my health around. I used to get migraines that left me in bed for a day or two or rather in bed for one day and worthless the next. Notice how I said, "used to." The truth is, I still get them but not as many, not as intense, and only occasionally. Believe it or not, changing my language to "used to" from "I get" made an incredible difference. I wasn't claiming my headaches. I wasn't giving them permission to be a part of my life. Does that seem a little out there? The power of words is a book in and of itself, and there are many books on the subject. Try it if you don't believe me. Watch your language and notice when you are negative. Try to give the thought a positive spin before you say it. It will make a profound difference in a very short time. I digress ... back to the playground.

So how did learning to play rid me of my migraines? I was an Army brat growing up, and there were more "boot-straps, young lady" than pampering. Not whining about it, it is just how it was. So that is what I did as an adult. I had a full-time job and went to school at night with no time to rest, let alone play. I controlled my body; my body didn't control me. "Boot-straps, young lady; soldier on; Army strong." Perhaps you know the motto.

When I was in my 20s, I had my tonsils removed, my gallbladder removed, and had constant headaches. Soldiering on wasn't working for me. My body was trying to tell me something and it was time I listened or work myself into an early grave. When I felt a headache come on, instead of telling it who was the boss and ignoring it until I couldn't, I stopped what I was doing and relaxed. I slowed down; I listened, I meditated, I laid down on the couch for a short time. Instead of losing two days to a full-blown migraine, I lost 30 minutes. Then I realized I didn't lose anything. The 30 minutes wasn't just a step I needed to take to get rid of my headaches; it was time well spent. It was the time that my body needed to recover. The lightbulb went off. Wow, if I just took the time upfront, then the headaches wouldn't "need to communicate" with me by shutting me down for two days, forcing me to crawl into bed so my body could rest and restore. That's when I learned to play.

Taking time to play also brought new friends into my life. Up until then, my only friends were co-workers. That is not a bad thing, but it can make you more rounded if you bring in people with other interests outside of work. Let's face it, a lot of gatherings with work friends end up being bitch sessions about work. Doesn't do much for raising the vibration and finding joy in life. Now my circle of friends includes people I met by taking agility classes with the pups and by joining racquetball teams, writing groups, and hiking clubs, to name a few. Don't get me wrong; I love my work friends. My dearest and closest friends are people that I met at work, but I also have a different set of friends that I would have never met had I stayed the "all work and no play" prior version of me. Taking time to play and have new experiences has brought joy, deep belly laughs, and a sense of community that I wouldn't trade for anything, especially not one more rung up the corporate ladder.

CHAPTER ELEVEN: Stop and Smell the Bluebonnets

Your life will be much more memorable if you stop and smell the flowers. Okay, I didn't get this one from Cooper & Max, but doesn't Cooper look cute?

When I lived in Texas, we couldn't wait for the Bluebonnets. There was a short window of time to take pictures and enjoy their beauty before the heat hit and they withered back. Every year we would take the pups to a local field and snap away, just like all the other families in Texas. We tried to find a spot that wasn't trampled on and tried not to add to the trampling. It wasn't always easy. Looking around at the families snapping away at their little angels, I noticed no one was enjoying the flowers. Tensions were high and the kids were getting restless waiting for that perfect shot. Mothers were yelling at dads to take the shot from a kneeling angle or move over to that tree nearby. I'm sure the resulting shots were gorgeous, but what about the opportunity to stop and smell the flowers? Was that lost or was it just a quick scratch and sniff and on to the next errand on the list?

This one is right up there with taking the time to play. There is more to stopping and smelling the flowers than a quick sniff. Stopping to smell the flowers is about being fully present and appreciating the flowers and having gratitude for them. Don't just smell the flowers, be with them, look at them, feel them. Notice the color, the details, the patterns, the beauty. Take it all in. Do you see how the experience is different, fuller, than a quick scratch and sniff? Now do this with everything in your life. Don't inhale your meals in front of the television. Set the table, arrange the silverware, savor the smell and the taste. Make it an active, meditative experience. You will be glad you did.

I got a ton of bruises before I learned this one and I don't mean figuratively. Until I learned this lesson, I was rarely present with the task at hand. My friend Sioux used to say, "get your seat in your seat" when she would see me drifting off in thought. Meaning get back in your body. Where did the bruises come from? I used to think I was accident-prone. Just check my childhood medical records and you might come to the same conclusion. Well, I wasn't accident-prone. I was "not-present-prone." What do I mean by that? Not being present and in the moment, I wasn't acutely aware of my surroundings. For example, when I would meet a friend for lunch to play racquetball, I would be timing how long it would take to shower, get in the car, and drive back to work so that I wouldn't exceed my hour. I wasn't fully enjoying the game. As soon as the match was over and before we walked out of the room, I was already thinking about the shower and my drive back. I would inevitably walk into the door on my way out of the court, bruising my arm. My husband used to say "can you put something with sleeves on when we go out? It looks like I beat you." The lesson is be present and aware of your surroundings. You will see more, feel more and have richer memories. For me being present and looking at my surroundings not only made the experience more memorable and richer, but it also kept me from looking like I was a member of a fight club.

  I take it back, Cooper and Max are very much about this chapter. They each have their favorite toy and, among those toys, chewing on a deer antler raises above all the others. They have a few they can select from. They go over to their basket of toys, smell for their favorite, and trot off to their beds to enjoy quiet time with the antler. They are so focused on chewing and holding the antler between their paws that I could drop a pot and they wouldn't budge. They are in the moment and loving every minute of it.

CHAPTER TWELVE: Pamper, Pamper, Pamper

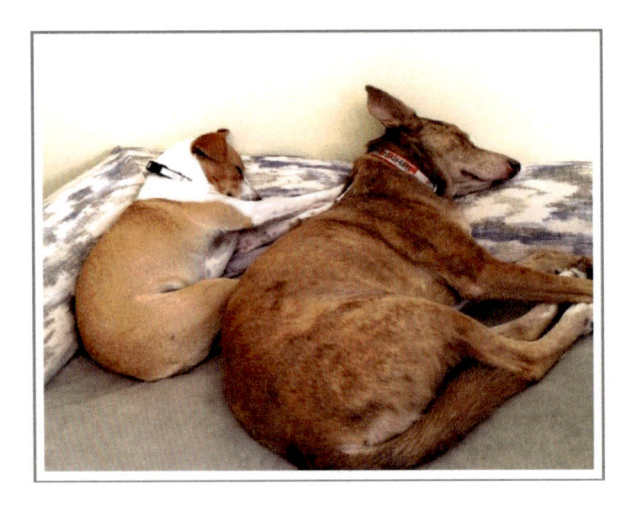

Please pamper yourself and I don't mean with a diaper. As women, we rarely put ourselves first, let alone pamper ourselves. I was a massage therapist and had more than one new client start sobbing on the table when I would ask them questions about how they felt about some story they were sharing. Why the tears? I think it is because most had never asked themselves how they felt about anything. Even something as simple as what they wanted for dinner. They always asked their family what they wanted to eat, the husband what movie he wanted to watch, and the kids what they wanted to do over the weekend. Having someone ask what they wanted or how they felt was startling and hit a nerve. I think it was also the feeling of being nurtured on the massage table when they were the ones always doing the nurturing.

To be fair, men need to pamper themselves as well. I think they may even have a harder time. It is socially acceptable to have a night out with the boys, which is invaluable for releasing stress, but often taking time out for massage or just opening up on an emotional level can be difficult because they may fear being perceived as not being strong.

I'm sure most of you have heard people use an analogy based on the opening lines of the airlines' "how to survive a crash" speech. It's probably going off in your head now. "Put your mask on first and then assist your child or the person next to you acting like a child." The "put your mask on first" applies to your daily life as well as when you are waiting for the oxygen mask to fall. Just as you are no help to your child if you are passed out because you didn't get your mask on time, you're not as helpful to your family if your energy is spent and you are exhausted.

If you can afford it, I highly recommend regular massages. If you can't, there are so many ways you can pamper yourself. Draw a nice lavender bath, take a walk in the woods, listen to a guided meditation, go to lunch or dinner with a friend, or just block out time to read a book from your favorite author. Better yet, take a page from Max and Cooper's book and just take a nice long nap!

CHAPTER THIRTEEN: Gratitude

That's Summer and Monty in the picture; I love Monty's face and overwhelming gratitude that he is going to share in our Thanksgiving feast.

Max and Cooper get a treat every night at 8:00. They expect it and Cooper knows how to tell time. At 7:59, you get the stare. If you haven't moved to pick up his Kong by 8:00, he will take his paw and tap your leg, just in case you didn't know what time it was. He expects it, but is still grateful. When you hand him his treat, he bounces to the den like he has just won the Lotto. Every time. Okay, I'm projecting, he probably doesn't have gratitude but you know what I mean.

Having gratitude for the blessings in your life keeps you in a positive frame of mind versus focusing on what you feel is wrong in your life. I didn't understand gratitude when I was younger. I remember when I was in high school, a college-age neighbor told me how grateful she was that God got her to school that day. She was short of money, the school was a few miles out, and it was raining. She said she found money in the sofa cushions and was able to ride the bus. I remember thinking, "you should be thanking the bus driver," never connecting that "finding the change" was a gift from God/Universe. (you pick)

Gratitude is a recognition that you have many things in your life to be grateful for and I don't mean stuff. I mean feeling supported, being able to shift a negative experience to an opportunity for growth. A negative experience like losing a job, may be what is needed to redirect you to a better opportunity that you may not have taken if you stayed in your comfort zone. I had something happen to me the week I wrote this chapter and thought that this is without a doubt a gift from God's hand to mine. I was certain of it; and boy was I grateful.

The lesson? Taking time to reflect on what you are grateful for changes your perception and can shift your entire day and how you react. Don't just focus on the big ticket items like a new promotion, but reflect on the little things as well. It will make them more memorable. I think having a practice of gratitude allowed what I'm about to share with you to happen. If I behaved like a spoiled, narcissistic brat with no gratitude, I am confident that I would still be blocked and struggling with fixing my presentation. Instead, I took a deep breath and said, I need some help here. So here is what happened. You decide; gift or just dumb luck. I know this is for some going to seem minor, but for me it was huge.

    I was building a presentation for work, and part of that presentation included two different charts showing values for life policies and values for health policies. I routed my first draft for feedback. There was a request to combine the two charts and to add a comma to the data, so the thousandth place was separated. Easy enough, or so I thought.

    I went back to the software I used to create the charts and tried to join the two charts. It was a disaster. It made everything go amuck and it pulled in information I didn't need. To top it off, the result was too large to paste into a new presentation. What was worse, adding the comma made the colored bar underneath the figure disappear. I panicked because I knew the person that asked for the comma really wanted it. I spent a few hours messing with it. Nothing worked.

I started practicing a speech in my head about why the charts couldn't be combined and that I wouldn't be able to add a comma on the original slides either. I was stressing. I decided to click on an old chart labeled "Life" to see if I could figure out what code was used to pull the "Life" data in so I could combine it with the Health chart. Low and behold, the chart labeled "Life" was a chart that was a combination of the Life and Health values and guess what ... it had commas! Sweet baby Jesus. I must have created this version a few years back before the charts were built separately. I don't think it was dumb luck that I decided to open that old file. I think I had a nudge to open it. I knew that was a gift from God and hollered out, THANK YOU! I found myself jumping around the office like I had just won the Lotto, hands held high in a victory dance.

CHAPTER FOURTEEN: Enjoy Moving

Max is so good about racing around the yard and running around the house with his toys. He loves it; you can see the joy spilling out of him.

Photo by Jim Antich

    Max has shifted my thinking on exercise. It's not just about moving; it's about loving that you are moving. I'm still working on getting more exercise but I'm following Max's lead, and I pick activities I love. I live across the street from the most beautiful trail and walking it is such a peaceful experience. It combines my pamper "me time" with exercise. I also picked Zumba. I love the music, I love the dancing, and I love how everyone laughs and has a good time.

    Pick something you love so exercise is something you get to do, not something you have to do. You are less likely to make excuses about why you can't fit it in. I won't bore you with the health benefits; you have heard all that before.

CHAPTER FIFTEEN: Get Those ZZZZZZs

I wasn't kidding when I mentioned having a large number of pictures of the pups sleeping. It seems like that is all they do, and I'll have to admit I'm envious. I have had trouble sleeping for years and finally broke down and signed up for a sleep study.

I learned a lot in that study. I knew not getting enough sleep affects your mood and your ability to concentrate. I was proof of that. I didn't realize the inability to focus could be dangerous. The office had posters showing that driving sleepy is just as dangerous as driving drunk. Makes sense, but I never made the connection.

What I was surprised by was my doctor's comment that I might lose 20 pounds if I started sleeping better. What? It has to do with a hormone. Not getting the proper amount of shut-eye causes hormone levels to drop. There is a hormone that plays a role in sending signals that you are full and when it drops, so does the signal, and not only are you hungry all the time, you crave foods that have a higher fat and calorie content. Who knew? Get you some ZZZs!

CHAPTER SIXTEEN: Teamwork

Max gets into everything. He is a chewer and is very stealth about it. Once Max chewed the shoe laces off my shoes while I was wearing them and I didn't notice until I stood up to go to the kitchen. He ate the strap off of my sister's shoe while she was wearing it as well. She was talking to a friend and thought he was just snuggling her foot. Next thing I know, we were off to the shoe store to buy her a new pair.

The power of teamwork: there is no way Max can reach some of the things he gets a hold of, so I knew there was some teamwork going on. I just didn't know to what extent until I walked into the kitchen one day and caught sweet Cooper in the act. Cooper is a counter surfer and I got a shot of it.

I'm not sure if Cooper's legs are spring-loaded or if he is standing up on Max's back to get on the counter. That would be real teamwork if Max helped him up. Before Max joined our family, Cooper never chewed or destroyed anything. That is no longer the case. I think Max talks him into bringing something down from the counter so Max can inspect it and the next thing you know, Max is knee-deep in destructive joy. How could Cooper possibly resist?

Okay, so I gave an example where teamwork can lead to destructive behavior and I think you will agree by watching the media that people in groups tend to behave differently than when alone. Someone might not throw a brick at a business window on their own, but when hidden in the anonymity of a group, the brick flies high and hard.

So that is the darker side of teamwork. What is the good side? The good side goes back to my comment on the power of women as a group. Think about the times you worked on a team either in sports or at work. You had a common goal or dream; you had people with different strengths that could bring that vision to a reality that you may not have been able to complete on your own or it would have taken forever.

Teamwork is also coming together as a community. I moved to Oregon from Texas so I didn't have lots of experience with snow. Apparently, neither does Portland. The town shuts down with a dusting of snow. Thankfully, I work from home. On the days we received snow, I didn't have to get in traffic and watched it from the sidelines. Watching the evening news was so inspiring. I watched the Portland community come together to handle a crisis that was shutting down the town. You would see video after video of people coming out of their homes with shovels, helping strangers dig their cars out of the snow when they got stuck in the street.

    For anyone who tries to do it all, you can't. It is impossible. Ask for help; it's not a sign of failure; it is the reality of life. There are only so many hours in the day, so many days in the week. You get it. Reach out, build a team and let us support each other along our respective journeys.

CHAPTER SEVENTEEN: Brotherly Love

I love watching Max. He is so affectionate and is always kissing Cooper and sleeping on him. If I added every picture I have of the two of them kissing and sleeping together and just generally being affectionate this book would be as thick as a War and Peace novel.

First let me say, I'm not a person that hugs everyone and, going back to that military background, I'm not a big kumbaya-around-the-fire kind of gal. I used to think people that needed affection all the time were needy. That is so not the case.

Reading *The 5 Love Languages* I referenced in an earlier chapter made me realize it is an important language to many, so I became a hugger, and I love it.

I realized that being affectionate helps keep me connected to my spouse. He gives hugs freely, leans in for snuggles, and is the most affectionate person I know. You see so many couples sitting at the same table but disconnected. One is reading text messages and the other is making a call. It is easy to get disengaged. Showing affection, sliding your hand across their back when you pass in the hall, touching their shoulder when you ask a question, or a quick kiss hello or good-bye brings that connection back each time and reminds you that you are not alone in this world.

CHAPTER EIGHTEEN: Always Learning

One of my favorite "I've got your back" photos.

I hope you had as much enjoyment reading through these God-guided, tail-wagging inspirations as I did in watching them unfold on a day-to-day basis. It could be argued that I am projecting human emotions and traits onto my animals, and perhaps I am. I've learned to watch their body language just like they watch mine. I might be projecting but I am okay with that. My heart is also open to gifts I receive every time one of these sweet angels enter my life. My time with each one is too short, but the lessons last a lifetime and I intend to honor those lessons by being the person my dog already thinks I am. It is the least I can do to repay them for their unconditional love and trust.

ABOUT THE AUTHOR

Joyce lives in Portland, Oregon, with her husband Michael, her two dogs, Cooper and Max and her two cats, Cassidy and Sissy. Cooper and Max continue to inspire Joyce on a daily basis.

This is Cooper's second starring role. He is the inspiration for a fictional dog, aptly named Cooper, in *Walk-In Investigations: Streaming Sarah A Paranormal Detective Mystery*. Cooper is the trusty sidekick of Detective Katie Hanson, a psychic detective. It is the first in a planned series. Maybe Max will show up in the sequel?

Made in the USA
Middletown, DE
27 June 2018